THE OPEN MOMENT

THE OPEN MOMENT

Reflections
on the
Spiritual Life

Swami Chetanananda

Rudra Press ⌒ *Portland, Oregon*

Rudra Press
PO Box 13390
Portland, OR 97213
Telephone: 503-235-0175
Telefax: 503-235-0909

Edited by Joan Ames
Book and cover design by Bill Stanton
Cover photo by Gary Hush Photography

Library of Congress Cataloging-in-Publication Data

Chetanananda, Swami
    The open moment: reflections on the spiritual life / Swami
Chetanananda.
        p.   cm.
    ISBN 0-915801-52-3
    1. Spiritual life—Quotations, maxims, etc.   I. Title.
BL624.C4526   1995
294.5′44—dc20   95-19822
                                                    CIP

00 99 98 97 96 95   10 9 8 7 6 5 4 3 2 1

Contents

Foreword

The Open Moment represents more than twenty-five years of Swami Chetanananda's ongoing endeavor to convey in words the depth of his own understanding and experience of the divine. The truths that he shares with us are the same basic truths taught by all authentic spiritual teachers down through the centuries. This universal wisdom cannot be limited or bound by any particular religious system. In the open moment one moves beyond all systems into a state of perfect clarity and luminosity where all truths manifest. The author speaks to us from that open moment.

These quotations, gathered from the last several years of Swami Chetanananda's lectures to spiritual students, have been selected both for their universal wisdom and their intrinsic power to convey simple truths. While the individual quotations are loosely arranged into twelve concepts that are basic to any spiritual path, one central and luminous message can be found in passages from all of the chapters. The effect is rather like a multi-faceted crystal that readers can turn in their hands: the basic teaching is extremely simple, yet it can be explained and clarified from many angles.

The essence of Swami Chetanananda's teaching is that all life experience arises from and subsides into one source. We have only to look within ourselves and into the other to find that source.

His simple directive to us as spiritual seekers— the basic teaching which shines through every facet of the crystal—is to release our tensions, open our hearts, and allow our own creative vitality to flow.

> The real worship and the only one that brings you any authentic growth as a spiritual person is the worship of opening your heart and deeply, from the core of your being, loving God every single day with every breath you take. Real devotion is doing this day after day for the rest of your life. It is this simple worship that cuts through all philosophical theories, transcends every religion and every distinction of gender, race, and nationality.

This fundamental strategy for spiritual growth is presented from various points of view in almost every chapter, and it is hoped that readers will benefit as much from dipping into *The Open Moment* at random as they would by reading the book from beginning to end.

There is a subtle logic to the order of the chapters. The first four chapters, *Growing, Vital Force, Spiritual Work,* and *The Teacher,* speak to the basic concepts that we need to understand and practice in our spiritual life. The middle four chapters, *Commitment, Pain, Mind,* and *Ego,* address the challenges that arise when we make a commitment to profoundly transform our lives. The final four chapters, *Love and Devotion, Service, Surrender,* and *Liberation,* represent the heart of our spiritual work and its goal.

Swami Chetanananda makes it very clear, however, that there is no "cookbook" that can guide a person through a series of orderly steps on a spiritual path. An open moment may bring the experience of liberation at any point in the spiritual journey. Therefore the book could also begin, rather than end, with the chapter on liberation. Similarly, devotion, service, and surrender are keys to growth that a spiritual person should understand and practice from the very beginning. In that light the chapters in this book can be read in any order.

The reader will notice that Swami Chetanananda uses a variety of terms to refer to that which most of the Christian world calls God. He doesn't use "God" exclusively because he feels that many people misunderstand this word or associate it only with the personified aspect of the divine. In his lectures to students, he makes it clear that he is not talking about some white-haired, fatherly figure sitting in heaven. He wants us to focus instead on the power of God within us, and ultimately on the experience of the Presence of God within. Although his use of language is always alive and fluctuating, his most recent teachings have included the following terms for God within: vital force, the ultimate, the Self (as distinct from self with a small "s"), the essence of life, creative energy, love, the absolute, and creative power.

Whatever religion you follow, whatever spiritual

practices you turn to each day, this collection of quotations from the talks of Swami Chetanananda should both guide and inspire you in living a truly spiritual life.

Joan Ames
Editor

Growing

❧ The wish to grow, to evolve and mature into the finest person we can possibly be, is one of the fundamental driving forces behind any extraordinary life—certainly any spiritual life. We only get out of life what we're willing to demand from ourselves, and if we want to attain our highest potential, growing will have to be our number one priority.

❧ In its most intense and powerful form, this wish to grow does not include any personal agendas or desired outcomes. We understand that our minds are too limited to conceive of the greatness we might become or the ways in which that greatness might unfold in our lives. In fact, there is no finer wish because we are surrendering all of our desires and limitations into the hands of God.

❧ The words themselves, "I wish to grow," when deeply felt, plant a seed in us which has within it the power to completely transform our lives. While this transformation is wonderful, it is also a challenge. Real growth brings us face to face with uncertainty, testing our strength, our commitment, our flexibility, and our trust in Life itself. The alternative—staying the same—is unthinkable to a person who truly wants to know God.

In your life and in mine there is a miracle that is available if we are willing to change and grow by opening to our highest potential. To do this we have to really care about the quality of our own life; we have to be willing to reach through our tension and confusion every day to connect to the finest part of ourselves. If we choose to engage and nurture that potential, it will grow and transform our whole life.

Where does the inspiration to grow and live an extraordinary life come from? When, for whatever reason, the clouds of tension within us have parted and we feel something special within ourselves, something which is beyond every kind of tension, worry, and problem, which is even beyond words—these are the times when we feel most alive. This experience is a great joy and a great release which powers our commitment to connect to and nurture that possibility within us again and again.

Instead of being totally attuned to opportunities to stay the same, develop the capacity to focus on and embrace real opportunities for growing. That's when life becomes a discovery process permeated with miracles.

Growing is real work. As you change, the process is going to bring about uncertainty, confusion, anxiety, and a lot of smoke and dust. It is certainly going to challenge all of your assumptions about yourself, about your friends, and about the direction of your life. Growing will challenge your attachments to just about everything and in the process teach you a lot about yourself. It's going to teach you a lot about the power that exists within you, about love and its individual and universal aspects. This is an endeavor that is worth a lifetime.

Growing is difficult. Everything else is impossible.

When we have an authentic longing and passion for growing we have an alternative to the pain and the stress of living. Our deep commitment to grow is a very simple, clear place from which to start every single day. We have something to turn to which is not a denial of anything but is rather a recognition that within all the misfortune and suffering of life, there *is* something which is authentically valuable, meaningful, and constantly uplifting and enriching.

The wish to grow leads us to see deeply into the reality of what we are and to recognize something extraordinary within ourselves. Because we invite it to grow, this most extraordinary part of us can expand, break through our tensions, and begin to manifest as the special Life within our lives—the Self of our selves—with a power and direction of its own. This Life within us is an inspiration which we can only serve.

In every situation we encounter, there are opportunities for growing and opportunities for creating tension. The whole situation turns on where we are within ourselves. It doesn't matter where anybody else is. Let the whole world be exactly where it is: complicated and confused. Then let us live within ourselves above the complication and confusion even as we move through it every day. Then really and truly we are totally transformed and released from amazing amounts of suffering.

Growth has its own life. It has its own voice, its own song, and its own manifestation. To attend to that growth and to bring that song out from within you may break you. And if it does, I say, "*boddhisvaha*" which means "hail the goer." To have the opportunity to truly grow is, in my view, the greatest treasure that life presents to us.

Our capacity to grow as a person is dependent on our ability to deal creatively with the turmoil of change. There is a difference between change and growth. Change is inevitable; growth is not inevitable. Change happens and is part of life; growth transcends change. If we want to grow, we must embrace the potential for growth that exists for us in every change.

Real growth takes place when we shed patterns of tension, when we drop intolerance, attitudes, prejudices, and desires. As we release those boundaries, we discover our capacity to encompass more and more of that which is all God's creation.

Spiritual growth is the process of seeing through and overcoming all of our fears and illusions about life in order that we can become stripped of our complexities, stripped down to the very simplest vibration that exists within us — the vitality, the pulse of Life itself, the breath of God. To discover and realize the fullness, the vastness, and the simplicity of that subtlest inner vibration releases us from our fears about gaining and losing and allows us to find within ourselves the logic of our own individual existence. We find our true place in the world and that place is within ourselves.

Once we commit ourselves to spiritual growth there is no day in our lives when we arrive at a place where we're complete and that's the end of it. The understanding that we're never finished growing is a wonderful thing. It can liberate us from our past, who we think we are, and all our limited approaches to life. Growing allows us to leave all our boundaries behind for something finer than we could ever imagine.

Growth is not in the future. It is in the present and in our ever-expanding awareness of the divine presence in each and every moment.

What we aspire to in spiritual growth is the ability to go through difficult experiences with our hearts open and full of devotion to the highest creative power. In that lived through experience we are transformed. Our limited understanding, our ego, our arrogance, our insecurity, and our fears are dissolved as we begin to realize the boundless qualities of our own essence which is the essence of Life itself. ∾

Vital Force

∽ When we turn our attention inside during spiritual practice, we become increasingly sensitive to our inner rhythms and the pulsation of vital force—our own essence and the essence of all of life. As we focus on this force and cultivate our experience of it, we develop the ability to feel its vibration and fluctuation at both the physical and subtle levels.

∽ At the physical level, vital force is the energy that powers our breath and other biological rhythms. With practice it is experienced as a flow of energy moving along the spinal column, a pulse that occurs twelve times a minute in healthy individuals. As we learn to stay attuned to the flow of vital force we find it washing away our tensions, improving our health, and filling us with well-being.

∽ At the subtlest levels this flow becomes the experience of the divine Presence where all levels merge into one luminous pulsation of consciousness—dynamic stillness. Here we pass beyond words into the ultimate mystery.

When we study the great spiritual traditions, we come to realize that all the names for the divine ultimately mean the same thing. We can call it love, holy spirit, God, Allah, nirvana, the ultimate, kundalini, chi, or vital force. It doesn't matter; it is all one.

Ultimately there are no words to describe it, no concept that can grasp it, and no form that can contain it. There is only the continual opening of ourselves to meet this vastness which is both nothingness and fullness at the same moment. It is nothing and everything all at once.

Vital force functions on every level of our existence. It is the health of our body, the stability and joy of our mind, the light of our intellect. It is the fullness of our heart and fundamental strength of our being. It is the life of our life.

There is no doctrine, no dogma, and no belief system which can express the vastness, the power, the simplicity, or the refinement of vital force. It is the essence of life in all of its incredibly diverse forms.

There is nothing we can intellectually grasp about vital force. There are no ideas that are relevant and ultimately every idea we do have about it is going to obstruct us. There is only the very simple pure experience of the fluctuation of vital force within us and its extension throughout the whole field of our life.

Consciousness and vital force are the same: we are conscious because of vital force, and we recognize that vital force because we are conscious.

As a spiritual person we become aware of our self as vital force. We take a breath, open our heart, and feel the flow and the pulsation of vital force within us. As our awareness of it grows, we will feel it expanding and changing its frequency, becoming finer and finer. If we stay attuned to vital force over time, our ability to follow it into the finest and broadest ranges of *its* capacity will wake up and grow.

To be really free, we must steadfastly cultivate vital force under difficult circumstances. We must do it for a whole lifetime, because basically life is like that—it's full of difficulties, hard work, and often a lot of pain and suffering with absolutely no guarantee about the outcome. It is only our connection to vital force that fills us with well-being even in difficult times.

Vital force has to do with a dimension in us that transcends all struggle, that is an infinite resource in our lives. In that infinite resource there is *right now*, and for infinity, no absence of anything.

To struggle with our material circumstances or emotions or ego is to deny ourselves access to this infinite resource. Unless we can penetrate the envelope of tensions that we have accumulated, we'll never experience vital force in operation. We will miss it because it is so simple, so subtle, so fine.

Vital force has no past, no problem, and no limitation whatsoever. It is the mind that has limitations. Vital force has no future and no need. It has no purpose; it simply is.

It is not by identifying with the trauma that we dissolve it. We dissolve trauma by identifying with the flow of vital force. It's very simple: don't worry or struggle. Don't identify with the frustration, or the tension, or whatever is bothering you. Identify with the flow. Vital force has the ultimate capacity to dissolve all traumas and deliver health and well-being to every level of our existence.

The resolution of every issue is found in more flow, whether it's physical injury or some kind of unhappiness, or mental or physical imbalance. By focusing on bringing the energy through ourselves and cultivating a flow, we change the pattern of our chemistry, our experience, and our whole life. It is the flow that opens our heart, awakens our sensitivities, dissolves our tension, and allows us to be more competent human beings.

More than anything else, the real test of our spiritual life lies in how we handle adversity. The point of spiritual practice is to build within ourselves such a deep connection to vital force that we are able to live above the ordinary tensions that plague most people. When life presents us with adversity, that connection allows us to live above our limitations and maintain our connection to that deepest creative power.

Vital force grows on its own and at its own rate, so we need to be patient. We can focus on our breath more and wish to grow more deeply, but we won't get vital force to grow any faster. What we *can* do is create an environment in which vital force will certainly grow much stronger, in which there will be space for it to expand enormously. It is the refined environment within us that we sustain that determines the strength, the reach, and the range of this dynamic occasion.

Vital force has the power to make you whole and to make your life completely full. It dissolves your desires, fills up your heart, washes away your ego, and exposes to you its own creative capacity in every direction you turn. From the continuous contemplation of this very simple pulsation of vital force within you, you are transformed and experience what it is to be one with God. ❧

Spiritual Work

∾ When we become really committed to a spiritual practice, we naturally have an appetite to
work harder and more continuously. Then doing
our regular practice once a week or once a day or
even twice a day does not satisfy. If we are sincere
about developing self-mastery and leading a spiritual life, we find opportunities to practice everywhere all day long. Then our spiritual work takes
on ever finer and broader dimensions as we learn to
sustain and cultivate our connection to the divine.

∾ Spiritual work is both joyful and painful,
sometimes calling on every last ounce of our determination to persevere. It is definitely work, and it
takes continuous practice. However, the rewards of
this work are completely stacked in our favor and
we end up getting back far more than we could
ever give.

In spiritual work there is probably only one commandment: know thyself.

Whatever our religious tradition may be, and wherever we come from on the face of this earth, our spiritual work is to see through the personal into the infinite and to understand the total interconnectedness of the two. The challenge of our life is to see God even in the personal, to understand that the very essence of what we are and what the next person is and what passes between us is God.

It is not just our regular attention to a spiritual practice that transforms us. So much of our growth comes from taking the understanding and experience we derive from our practice and integrating it into our everyday lives. Eventually there will be no separation between our spiritual work and our work in the world.

As spiritual people our practice is to keep our
hearts open in every situation. This calls for
total determination. When we find ourselves
closing we don't just lie down, roll over, and get
tangled up in whatever mind bramble has taken
over. Basically, we whack it down and make the
effort to establish again a condition of openness
and connection to the flow of vital energy in and
around us.

Our work is to understand that everything is
of one essence. We don't criticize or judge
anything. This understanding creates tolerance
and real respect for all diversity. Through our
practice we cultivate an inner richness, an inner
strength, an inner clarity, and a largeness of
heart and spirit that manifests as true love and
respect for everybody.

Certainly there are profound benefits to all aspects of our lives that arise from spiritual work, both in the short term and in the long term. However, we don't do this work to get benefits. Spiritual work is not about feeling better. Spiritual work is about knowing the truth and there is something both discomforting and exhilarating about living in contact with the truth.

If we don't use our practice, then it doesn't grow. Very simply, it is conscious work. In many instances spiritual work is incredibly joyful. On occasion it is filled with sadness and some terror as the totality of our being is transformed. Always it is work that gives back a thousand-fold what we put into it, but if *we* don't do it then it doesn't happen.

In spiritual work you open yourself to every level of your life. You open your heart to your pain, your suffering, your disappointment, your frustrations, and your fear of the unknown. Rise above the tensions and face your life straight up, eyeball to eyeball. Face it from your own center with your heart open so that you can slowly allow the whole field of your life to be filled with light, to be filled with love. Make something special out of each moment.

The most important thing we have to do every single day—the work of our work—is to lighten up and give of ourselves as much as we can. The more we put into the flow of life the more the flow comes back to us. That's the dynamic of the universal system.

The unfolding of love that comes with spiritual work does not give us certainty; it doesn't give us any answers. What it gives us is immense vitality and great joy.

It's only when we can work without ego, without attachment, and without expectation of some reward, when we can work every day with devotion—whatever work it is we are called upon to do—that the vision of God arises in the plane of our innermost awareness.

In infinity the time is now and the place is here. This is always true, no matter what. Even in the face of the ten million states of confusion that are ever present for us to fall into, if we really want to live a spiritual life in contact with God, the time is now and the place is here. There is no other.

As you move through your day, turn your attention continually to that dimension of your life which is truly rich, truly wonderful and powerful, and filled with total uncertainty. Turn your attention to that, not with fear but with openness and love. Allow that infinite domain to manifest its power in your life in ways that don't reinforce your tensions but instead release them. In this way you will transcend yourself and all your limitations.

The purpose of spiritual practice is to achieve a degree of communication with God that completely, totally fulfills us.

The heart of God is vast—unbelievable, beyond anything our minds can comprehend—and sweet.

We are closest to God when our hearts are open and there is a sense of sweetness and a little bit of joy in us. We cannot be filled with ourselves, totally self-absorbed, and absorbed into the heart of God at the same time. Two things cannot occupy the same space; it's simply not possible. Every day we get to choose which thing we want to be filled with; it's always and only our own choice. ∾

The Teacher

∾ When we decide to learn anything in real depth, the benefits of being in the physical presence of a skilled and qualified teacher are immeasurable. This is certainly true if we want to pursue a spiritual life. A great teacher will not merely serve as our instructor and guide on the spiritual path; such a person will be a source of inspiration, will put us in contact with the inner teacher, and will be able to impart to us the direct experience of the divine.

∾ Authentic spiritual teachers are very rare; when we find such a teacher we have found an extraordinary treasure, one that will certainly transform our lives.

A teacher is both a living vision of what we are working toward in our spiritual practice and an energy source that nourishes that transformation within us. This energy source and vision should give rise to devotion for our spiritual practice simply because we see that it works and is dependable. Devotion and trust, the vision of a possibility, give rise to our capacity to surrender and be transformed, to happily leave behind the familiar, to enter into a higher and finer state.

The purpose of any spiritual practice is to have a direct experience of God, of ultimate reality, and one of the most important elements in this endeavor is a spiritual teacher. The true teacher is neither the body nor the personality, but rather an energy source, a total field of information from which you can draw. The essence of spiritual work is to stay attuned and connected to that energy source. The transformation within us that results from this connection allows us to have the direct, one-on-one contact with the ultimate that we are seeking—that anybody who is serious about spiritual work is seeking.

In our spiritual work we try to connect to the energy field that is the teacher. That point of contact is the most sacred place in the whole universe.

One essential power manifests in the presence of a truly spiritual person—the power to open minds and melt hearts.

As we start to draw in the energy of a spiritual teacher, our own energy pattern changes. Energy that we absorb from the teacher ignites a subtle but real change in the temperature within us. This extra heat releases tensions and poisons within our muscles and our nervous system. Resources that are locked in our inner tensions become available and are slowly incorporated into the whole process of growing. This is a self-catalyzing process that feeds upon itself. As our energy increases more tensions are freed which gives us more energy to free more tensions. The process repeats itself until there is such a deep shift within us that suddenly a door opens and we see God.

The Teacher

It is important to understand that there's no such thing as a perfect teacher or a perfect person. It is only when we are able to open our hearts and encompass the differences, the imperfections, and the contradictions that exist in other people that we'll be able to really love ourselves. Only then are we free to see that perfection and imperfection are irrelevant and that underlying all behaviors there is a vitality which is rich and noble and powerful.

The real teaching is transmitted from heart to heart and soul to soul, not any other way.

You can't wrap your mind around a spiritual teacher. No concepts can be built that will help you truly understand a teacher, it is not possible. And yet, what an amazing experience it is to participate with an authentic teacher, and what amazing joy, challenges, work, and insights come from contact with a teacher.

The teacher is the greatest treasure, and it is free. It comes because you want it. It stays because you treasure it. It releases you because you love it. Find such a teacher, and when you do give yourself over completely.

Enduring in time and space—near or far, high or low—there is a continuous connection with the essence of the teacher which serves to uplift us in every single experience we have. The connection allows us to accept in a quiet way the disappointment of our material existence. This contact brings us the capacity to openly endure, with integrity, the breaking of our heart and sets the stage for us to move deeply into the dimension of pure spirit.

The real essence of the student-teacher relationship is the deep contact that establishes itself in the form of mutual love and respect. In this contact there exists a mutual sacrifice—the teacher sacrificing themselves into the student, the student sacrificing themselves into the teacher. In this sacrifice we are really giving of ourselves that we can grow and expand and come into contact with the beauty, the majesty, the mystery, and the miracle of life itself—the source of who and what we are and all that we see. It is a wonderful thing.

The key issue is not what kind of teacher you have, but what kind of student you are.

A great teacher is first and foremost a great student. Secondly, a great teacher is *continuously* a great student, otherwise their teaching is no longer a living presence. It's dead. We have to be committed to being students for our entire lives, and this commitment must come before everything else.

A teacher is available. That's all. A teacher doesn't want anything from us except that we should be our highest Self.

The real teacher is inside us. It is the energy which is going to teach us about itself. The physical teacher can arouse that energy and put us into a deeper contact with it for a little while; then it is up to us to pay attention to that energy so that it can teach us about its own creative power.

The teacher is nothing but that totally transcendent field of truth from which life arises and into which it subsides.

The connection to a spiritual teacher is a sacred thing. If there is anything in this universe that is sacred, *that* is sacred. Contact with a spiritual teacher is a very powerful thing. By becoming one with the vibration that is the connection, we truly promote our own transformation process.

Whatever obstacles challenge the development of that connection, we humble ourselves, we surrender ourselves, we do whatever it takes to maintain and cultivate the connection. In no way are we reduced in this process; by surrendering our ego and at the same time maintaining our contact with vital force, we become a much bigger person. The miracles that flow from our capacity to cultivate this connection are unfathomable. ❧

Commitment

❧ If we truly want to have a more extraordinary life, then we must find a more extraordinary place within ourselves to live from. The choice is ours and it is up to us to make it happen. Although some people may try to sell the easy spiritual trip, there are no angels that are going to come down and wave a magic wand over us, and presto, we're somebody else. All that sort of thing is delusion.

❧ It takes real commitment to walk through the experience of total transformation. The basic practice may be simple, but it is not easy. It takes work, work, and more work; it takes practice, practice, and more practice.

❧ We start exactly where we are and work from there. The more we practice and find it works, the deeper our commitment will become. This process sets up a powerful self-reinforcing mechanism that allows us to have real intensity and passion for our practice.

❧ Ultimately such a deep commitment is like a center of gravity within us: it keeps us firmly grounded in the work we need to do to be transformed; it allows us to use that work as a lever to lift ourselves above the tensions in our lives over and over again; it is the base from which we can become truly expansive.

As the Buddha sat down under a tree and said I'm not moving until I'm enlightened, we're sitting down within ourselves and opening our hearts and saying we're not budging from this place no matter what.

If we are to grow as human beings, it is essential that we have a deep, authentic, and unshakable commitment to that growth. Perhaps our commitment will show itself as participation in spiritual practices and organizations, but the real commitment is to mental clarity and emotional simplicity, it is to staying focused on our inner state and connected to the flow of vital force in our lives.

When we are totally committed to the process of internal awakening and can live every day from that feeling of commitment within ourself, we cut through all the confusion in our mind because our number one priority is established. Once we have that grounding in our first priority all other aspects of our life fall into place. In the presence of this deep commitment all our inadequacies evaporate.

Committed spiritual students, in their passion for understanding and abiding in the highest state, transcend every kind of judgment and doubt. They are able to give themselves up totally to attaining the ultimate.

Commitment is not about rigidity, fanaticism, or becoming contracted or closed in any way. We're not making a commitment to any ideology or person. Our commitment is to a state of being: to nobility, to virtue, and most importantly to growth and the expansion of our understanding. Commitment is a continuous awakening. It leads us to hunger and thirst for a deeper understanding of our own nature and the experience we are passing through.

The transitions we face in our lives often cause us to become agitated, scattered, and confused. In every transition there is a period of emptiness as the old thing, whatever it is, goes away and the new thing, whatever it is, has not yet emerged. If we have a real commitment to spiritual practice, we can pass through these periods of transition with inner peace and clarity, able to focus on what is going on and finding the real opportunities for growth.

If we really want to improve ourselves and deepen our understanding, there has to be in us a deep commitment to awaken and sustain that longing to grow. Some days we will have to reach through our tensions to find it. Commitment becomes a center of gravity around which our life starts to form and reform as tensions and limitations fall away. Every day we keep returning to that center of gravity, no matter what.

To become a great human being requires great commitment, determination, and the capacity to persevere. In spiritual practice, it is only because of our capacity to commit and persevere that we reach a deep place within ourselves long enough for its sweetness and its power to mature. That maturing creates a richness and a joy in us that is palpable to all and serves our fellow human beings in extraordinary ways. ∾

Pain

❧ In this world people spend tremendous amounts of time and energy trying to avoid pain. The problem with trying to insulate ourselves from pain is that we end up shutting out much of life along with powerful opportunities to grow into stronger and finer people. Ironically, it is usually the painful times in our lives that offer us the greatest lessons and hold out the truths we most need to know. If we truly want to grow and lead a spiritual life, we will learn to be open to pain and what it has to teach us.

❧ We don't have to go looking for pain; it comes on a fairly regular basis for most people. It is how we deal with pain that is always a true test of ourselves and how much we are evolving in our lives. Great people have learned to rise above pain and keep their hearts open even in the face of tremendous pressure.

The times when we are suffering are the most important times of transformation. During these periods of our life there is nothing else to do but calmly pass through the reorganization happening within us. The more we can rise above all the turmoil in our heads, and keep our hearts open, the more quickly and efficiently we arrive at an increasingly refined state within ourselves. Slowly we develop the ability to go through these painful periods without too much wear and tear.

If we are afraid of pain—it doesn't matter what kind of pain it is—we are in deep trouble. Whether it's the pain of the past or the pain of the present or the pain of the future, we are either above it, or we're caught in it. If we accept the idea that there is some pain that we should bow down in front of, then we will end up bowing down in front of all pain. Then pain is going be hurting us big time. We do not have to torture ourselves to get above pain; we have to be clear about our goal, drop the struggle, and open our hearts.

To be able to live in a state in which we are beyond the ups and downs and rounds and rounds of the endless merry-go-round of life, we will burn some, we will experience much agitation and a lot of discomfort and distress. In a way, the same pain we experience accumulating tensions we feel again as we get rid of them.

As we go through these periods of burning, the essential thing is that we have genuine devotion to achieving the highest state. Just the devotion that we feel to the highest is in fact the very essence of liberation. The simple joy that we feel in knowing that we have a choice, and that this burning is not forever, points the way to achieving a state that denies nothing and is the transcendence of everything.

Being a strong person is being able to take on the pain of life and keep your heart open.

Most people are busy seeking pleasure and avoiding pain, but in fact, it would be wise to take a second look at this approach to life. If we want to grow, pain is always going to be an important source of true and valuable information. Pleasure, on the other hand, is not such an honest friend. The pursuit of pleasure brings about a lot of trouble for all of us in our lives, and it is constantly feeding us delusion.

In order to become a truly big person with a big heart and a very much bigger mind, we may have to suffer a little bit, and that's the price we pay. Whatever it is we hope to achieve in our lives, we will definitely have to pay—not with money, but with blood, sweat, and tears. There is no such thing as a free lunch in this world, not one.

In spiritual practice we open ourselves to the flow of strong energy that is available to us in our lives. We are opening to that even though it hurts, because the hurting is nothing but our barriers and limitations dissolving in that flow of energy. Once we understand that, pain is not a problem.

To have our hearts open and filled with love is our greatest protection from any kind of harm in this life.

Most of the hurt that happens to us in life is really our own responsibility, not somebody else's. The hurt happens because we want something from somebody that they don't have, or we want something from life that isn't available. And in a way that is ridiculous because there is so much in life that is always available.

The complexity that emerges within our life experience is essentially a product of our own response to pain. Very much the way an oyster secretes a coating around a grain of sand to reduce the agitation and make itself more comfortable—at least temporarily, we create our own forms of insulation around life's pain which causes a kind of complexity to be established in our life. This insulation enables us to compartmentalize all the facets of our life and the discomfort within them. In so doing we set up and maintain a kind of crystallization which actually inhibits our growth. In our spiritual work we become aware of and release these points of crystallization in our life.

Sometimes opening ourselves up brings pain. It is not a natural thing to become more and more open; it is not something that society encourages or that most people attempt. In this openness we will continually confront some scary and painful things. We will start to see the parts of ourselves that we usually deny: our own inflexibility, our lack of sensitivity, and a whole range of limitations that we ourselves bring to our life. Beyond that we are going to discover the vastness of life itself and how unimportant we actually are.

But if we are to lead a spiritual life we just work and love and get hurt and open and love and work and get hurt some more. We keep opening and growing through it all until we become a truly vast and extraordinary person who has transcended all the tension there is to transcend and who lives a life of deep understanding and true compassion for all.

Everybody in this life has lots of difficulties to face, and when we start to feel angry about our life's circumstances it is good to step back a moment and ask who we should be angry at. Most people, the people we're mad at, are just victims of circumstance like us. So who's going to rise above all the tensions and become a whole person instead of living under this cloud of poison gas that most people call life on earth? We've all got plenty to be angry about. Life is pain and suffering as the Buddha made perfectly clear 2,500 years ago.

If we want to grow, there is no other choice but to keep our hearts open, to give back all of the insult and all of the injury and all of the stupidity, violence, and brutality—give it all back with love. We do this by living within ourselves from the light of that creative power which has poured forth this whole universe. It is this effort that makes us a big person and transforms our life into a really big life. ∞

Mind

～ Everyone knows what it is like to be at the mercy of their own mind. Our mind has the power to either uplift us or bring us down in a flash. It can also be a powerful tool when it is clearly focused and one-pointed.

～ In spiritual practice we learn to surrender the turmoil between our ears and move our attention to the flow of vital force. We do not struggle with the mind; we don't suppress, repress, or deny anything. The less energy we lock up in tensions, the more energy we have to nurture our deepest inner Self. Simply, we release the tension and focus our mind on the highest.

The mind is the key, the real leverage point, in sustaining the flow of vital force and our connection to God. Either we are opening our mind constantly and focusing it on the presence of the divine within us, or we are getting entangled in some form of limitation. It is only when we are one-pointed on the highest within us that we are released from the merry-go-round in our head.

The mind's incessant working, calculating, and recalculating totally undermines our ability to focus on vital force and its very simple, clear, beautiful fluctuation that, like the tide, carries us of its own accord to the other shore—the experience of life that transcends the mind and the body and the ego.

It doesn't pay to get convoluted and intellectual and caught up in our heads trying to make sense out of our lives, because life is not a sensible or rational event. The patterns of our lives cannot really be encompassed by the mind.

What we think we want is a trap. What we think we need is also a trap. Pursuing our wants and our needs only causes the limitations and tensions which we bring to our daily life to be further contracted and tightened around us.

It is important to remember that there is something in our lives that is vastly more profound and tremendously richer than anything that we could possibly want or imagine with our minds.

We can think of the mind as the fire which is constantly consuming all experience, and ultimately all experience is just nourishment for our growth as a person.

All too frequently the mind is simply a reactionary, justifying mechanism. It has the capacity to take what is potentially nourishment and structure it as tension, to reduce every experience to the lowest common denominator. In this way the mind is the slayer of the soul.

Basically the mind has one thought that it will carry to its grave: "What's going to happen to me?" This is the mind's fundamental and persistent chant that powers all of our individual issues, problems, hopes, and fears.

Instead of being caught in this endless loop of self-concern, we turn our mind and our whole being to the thought, "I wish to grow." With practice this wish takes us beyond all of our personal issues. We turn our mind to the flow of vital force, and to the best of our ability we don't let it go anywhere else.

When we free our minds from the need to understand, then suddenly the unexplainable is revealed and we can accept it. We don't figure it all out until we stop figuring. We don't achieve anything at all until we stop struggling and striving. There is something extraordinary in our hearts that flowers in an environment that is free of attachments, aspirations, and struggle.

The mind and the soul never exist separately or independently. It is the soul that gives life to the mind and the mind that illuminates the existence and the nature of the soul. In this case the mind is not a problem; the mind is really the vitality of the soul, the vitality of the individual. In a sense there is never any separation between mind and soul or between individual and God.

If you seek to know the boundaries of your mind, where will you find them? You may not. You may not find any boundaries. So maybe man and God aren't separate. And maybe our soul is the one universal Soul. Maybe each of us in our individual lives, like waves in an ocean, are expressions of that ultimate creative power, and we are each within ourselves connected to a resource, *always* connected to a resource which is truly profound. ❧

Ego

∽ Seeing the truth about our own ego is not usually an easy or comfortable process. We spend a lot of time building up and defending this "I" as if it had real stability and substance. In fact this "I" is really a process with very little real continuity other than the stream of stresses and strains that has shaped it.

∽ When we become committed to leading a spiritual life, to growing and opening ourselves to change and uncertainty, the ego reacts with fear and resistance. If we let this agitation dominate our awareness we will not only find change impossible, we will eventually cut off the nourishment for our spiritual development.

∽ The good news is that human beings are capable of remarkable personal evolution and change. If we look to the power behind the ego we come face to face with the same power that manifests this whole universe. In that vision and experience of the ultimate, the "I" is simply transcended.

The unpleasant, painful memories that we have
of past traumas in our life come from our ego.
When there is an opening inside us that presents itself as the potential for tremendous
change, the ego immediately floods that space
with memories of the past: "You were this, you
were that; these are all the things you were..."
Like the platelets in our blood which create a
sticky binding to close up a wound, this sticky
ego chemistry comes out to bind us together
whenever there is an opening, an uncertainty, a
space in which some new kind of creative force
might emerge. It's an ego trick.

When we think about our inadequacies and we get upset and we think about our past and we are upset, or we think about our present or our future and we get upset, what is it that we are actually upset with? Ultimately we're upset with God, aren't we? And ultimately, if we hang onto it long enough, what does that do? It creates tension between us and our own essence, it creates doubts around which our ego crystallizes. It is through our spiritual practice, through staying centered and connected to our deepest Self, that we naturally deal with these doubts and resolve them.

As the energy of our spiritual practice begins to power up our whole being, one of the things it's going to do initially is power up our ego as well. If we are to become a person with deep integrity and understanding, a person who respects themselves, then it will be necessary at various points to confront our ego. The ego is very tricky, and in confronting it, the only thing that will save us is our capacity to stay focused on our spiritual work.

When we are trying to grow spiritually the resistance we run into again and again comes primarily from ourself, from our ego which is essentially seeking glorification even in our attempts at self-improvement. The ego is amazingly flexible and has the capacity to absorb tremendous amounts of energy without ever really changing. The minute we start thinking that we have accomplished something, or that we're hot stuff and it is *our* doing, we are only reinforcing our ego. It takes hard work and a lot of humility to release our boundaries and the familiar sense of self in order that we can become attuned to a very much subtler voice that is speaking within us.

What if the self that we understood we were yesterday, was the person that we had to live with from now on? What if that were true? It wouldn't be pretty would it? It's a wonderful thing to be released from whom we think we are, because who we think we are is really a fabrication.

If we are wrapped up in our own ego then we're really only concerned about *getting*. Unfortunately, our concern about getting completely constipates us. The tension that builds around our concern to acquire this thing and that thing limits our capacity to absorb anything beneficial to our growth. The exertion simply limits our ability to take in, and the more we try the less we get.

It is only in giving ourselves away that we are constantly getting ourselves in an ever and ever greater dimension. It's only when we totally give ourselves away that we have the capacity to really know ourselves. ∾

Love and Devotion

～ When we are drawn to a spiritual life, the quest for love takes on a whole new direction and meaning. We are no longer limited to looking for love outside ourselves in some other. We learn to follow the love that we experience back to its source within ourselves.

～ We come to understand that love is the fundamental power of life which continuously nourishes and serves every human being and in which every human being finds their fulfillment. In love there is no need or absence of anything. Love has the power to transform lives, to restore health, and to bring about within us a sense of total well-being.

～ The goal of a spiritual life is simply to live in a state of love which not only fulfills us but becomes a source of inspiration to all the people our lives touch.

Awakening the fire of love and devotion within ourselves and cultivating that state will dissolve all the hardness in our hearts, burn up all the tensions, and make perfect clarity our everyday life state. Keeping that fire of love and devotion alive within ourselves is serious work, and it's wonderful work. The miracles that flow from this process are unfathomable.

I think devotion is the only sweet thing that exists in the world. Without devotion, spiritual commitment is a hard dry force that denies life experience, a force that may not have the power to absorb into itself the range of information that is necessary to transform us. It is devotion that turns our spiritual commitment into something that is alive, that breathes, and that encompasses all life experience.

The secret to becoming a stronger person is very simple, very clear, and in a way the whole point of every spiritual tradition. It's love. It's love. It's love. The love that we share is the power that makes us stronger. I'm not talking about just feeling love inside ourselves and thinking that we're strong. It's a love that has to be expressed and shared and participated in. It is devotion to that love, focusing on that love, being sensitive to the movement of that love within ourselves and among ourselves; it is engaging it and allowing it to happen that makes us stronger. Otherwise, nobody is easily a strong person.

The devotion that we feel to the highest is in fact the very essence of liberation.

Very simply, if we want love in our lives, we have to give love in our lives.

Devotion is not something that in any way reduces a human being. People sometimes think that devotion demonstrates a weakness—that we should be strong, meaning we should be totally closed and rigid and only concerned about ourself. To have any other concerns means we're weak. How stupid is that? What happens to anything rigid or concerned only with itself? It breaks.

The most important thing is to be devoted to our spiritual work because then every emotion can be transformed into a higher and finer state. Being really devoted is such a sweet thing; it makes our hearts very big and our whole life seem like a miracle.

Love never dies. Perhaps the forms will pass away; that which we could not absorb will pass away. Though sometimes painful, this passing away is a good thing; it keeps us healthy and growing. Love itself endures because it transcends form, it transcends time, and it transcends space.

Our capacity for surrender arises from devotion. If there is no devotion, then when the time comes to surrender we are only going to give up one set of tensions for another set of tensions. Devotion is the environment in which surrender takes place.

To really reach the highest state is an either/or proposition, in the same way that being an athlete who wants to reach the Olympics takes a serious commitment and a lot of hard work. Either we're doing the work or we're not going to reach our goal.

Spiritual work can only be sustained over time if we have authentic devotion. If there is no devotion then it becomes a chore. If there's no devotion there's no real potential for surrender, and if there's no potential for surrender, there's no growth.

We may think about love in terms of exchange— in terms of giving and receiving. At a certain point, though, as we look at it more carefully, we will start to understand that we are neither giving nor receiving anything. We are simply participating in the vitality of the Essence of life. *This* is what gives everything.

To discover a mature and universal love is to be beyond coming and going; it is beyond giving and getting. There is no gain and no loss, only a subtle, special sweetness which is accessible to us with every single breath of our life.

Have you noticed how love and pain always come together, one hidden inside the other? In experiences where love predominates there will be some pain, and in painful experiences there will also be some love and joy. No amount of intellectualizing is ever going to separate these two aspects of life or resolve the fundamental tension between them. In fact no resolution is necessary because it is not a problem.

Love, in its universal sense, is an infinite pouring forth and giving of itself. We think of pain as the opposite, as a kind of withdrawal or contraction. In all of life there is the endless fluctuation of extension and contraction. The inhalation is followed by the exhalation. The tide pours forth changing the structure of the beach and then pulls back to reveal the change. This tension between love and pain is simply part of the vital force from which the whole world flows. In growing spiritually we find our own balance first and then the balance between these two fundamental expressions of life: love and pain.

The real worship and the only one that brings you any authentic growth as a spiritual person is the worship of opening your heart and deeply, from the core of your being, loving God every single day with every breath you take. Real devotion is doing this day after day for the rest of your life. It is this simple worship that cuts through all philosophical theories and transcends every religion and every distinction of gender, race, and nationality. ∾

Service

∾ True service comes from the experience of the interconnectedness of all of life and the recognition that whatever we do for others we are doing for ourselves as well.

∾ Service is not in any way altruistic. It is our participation in that dimension in which every human being's highest best interest is one.

We're in this world to give something, not to get something. Our work is to discover what is within ourself that is worthy of giving, and then to give it.

True service has to do with our ability to relate to the living essence of any situation or human being. We do this work from a simple and deep place within ourselves, free of our ego and our agendas. When we relate from that deep place within ourselves to that deep place in other people, we are not just serving others. It is nice if someone else benefits, but in truth we are serving life itself.

Serving God is releasing tensions.

The work that we do in the true spirit of service is the only work we will ever do that never becomes crystallized or boring. Service is work that is ever new even as it is endlessly the same.

When we talk about service, we are not talking about being a nice person who volunteers a little time helping somebody else. Service is not doing things for people, or for getting credit or having people like us for what we've done. Service is releasing tensions and being aware of the flow of energy within ourselves and between us and everyone.

We serve because we need to serve, because it is an essential element in our spiritual development. Service is an opportunity to participate directly in the flow of vital force.

In leading a spiritual life, we give of ourselves as much as we can. The more we put into the flow of life the more the flow comes back to us. That's the dynamic of the universal system.

If we are serving authentically, we don't think about helping people, even if we are. Our focus is on helping ourselves by releasing tensions and allowing a flow of creative energy to unfold in the situation. If we do this sincerely and consciously, then our limitations and tensions will dissolve. A real and palpable love will come into our lives. It may not tell us what to do or how to do it, but this love comes from deeply within us, uplifting us and everyone we are in contact with.

Part of learning to serve authentically is to listen to ourselves and to the nonsense that rolls out of our mouths on occasion so that we can hear it coming before we start speaking. We can just be quiet. Instead of constantly talking about ourselves, we feel through our own tensions and insecurities *into* other people and their needs. We really become aware of the other person; we focus on them and feel the flow of creative energy in them and between us. Then we meet each person where *they* are, not where we are. This allows real love to be present and to mature.

In a way, service is a sophisticated attitude and understanding. It is not a denial of ourselves, ever. It should never cost us our integrity or our center. Rather it is an affirmation of our potential. In releasing ourselves into a situation, we are not extinguishing ourselves to do something for somebody; we are actually *expanding* our own center. We feel deeply within ourselves and feel the expansion of our own flow. In doing this we are encompassing other people and participating in their lives in a simple, profound way.

There are lots of simple ways to serve. When we are not self-absorbed, we see when something is needed and understand that responding to that with an attitude of service enriches the whole environment. Service is bringing a little more joy into everybody's life. It is a wonderful thing. ∾

Surrender

∾ Surrender is a concept that makes a lot of people nervous. They wonder what they are going to have to give up, and to whom. If we want to lead a spiritual life, the only thing we will ever have to give up is our own limitations. As we learn to relax and let go of tensions and worries and fears, we create an opening within ourselves that allows our own creative potential to expand. Surrender is the key to a deeper experience and understanding of our own lives and of the divine in all of life.

Surrender has nothing to do with letting go of our ideals and our principles. It is certainly not surrendering to anything or to anybody else. It is not even surrendering to God. It has only to do with letting go of our tensions, our fears, and our attachments so that the love in our heart can expand. It means letting go of anything that disturbs the flow of love in us, and consequently the flow of love in our life. We surrender the struggle so that we can connect to and be nourished by the divinity of our own essence. That is what surrender is.

You cannot hold on and let go at the same time. It is not possible. The whole discussion of attachment, or non-attachment begins with the understanding that without really letting go you can't grow, you can only stay the same. And, if you're holding on, you're not letting go. It's that simple.

Surrendering is relaxing into every moment. It is feeling deeply the flow and power of life within and around us. It is not having *a* feeling, or feeling emotion, but simply participating in the power of perception and developing our ability to feel. Releasing our thoughts and tensions, our worries, fears, and doubts—that is giving of ourselves, that is surrendering.

We may try, but we will definitely not benefit from surrendering things or experiences that aren't really ours. Surrender is also not about giving up the petty things we're attached to. It has everything to do with finding a deeper power within ourselves and releasing ourselves with faith and trust into the flow of that power. We do this without giving up our own discrimination or the responsibility that we have for our own lives. It's a very fine balancing act.

If we are empty, life will fill us up. If we are full, life will definitely empty us. We get to choose. If we think we are big, life makes us low. If we think we are small, life pushes us up.

We should think carefully about this so that humility and simplicity and emptiness become experiences we really understand. The ability to achieve emptiness is a powerful skill which will serve us in every moment of our lives.

Every day we empty ourselves of our concerns and become like an empty cup or an empty bowl, or if possible, like an empty ocean or an empty galaxy. We just become as expansively empty as we can. Then we wait for a while and see if some finer vibration doesn't begin to fill us up and overflow.

True change really manifests from a shift in a person's subtle state, and that change in subtle state only occurs as we let go, and let go, and let go. *The key is surrender.* We surrender what we want, we surrender our ego, we surrender our frustration, agitation, and confusion, we surrender whatever is needed to create that openness inside us in which change can manifest. There is no sustainable change of any state of being that can happen unless it is founded upon surrender.

Detachment is an essential spiritual value. It is necessary for us to truly detach from everything that comes and goes in our lives, because those things are going to do just that: come and go. If we can't rise above the surface level of tensions in our lives on a regular basis, if we can't stay detached from all the coming and going, then we are too busy being consumed by the drama to learn anything. We are pouring ourselves into nothing, into a storm that just blows and blows and goes nowhere.

Surrender is the environment in which total transformation takes place.

The depth of our spiritual awareness and understanding is based upon surrender, and ultimately that surrender extends even to giving up growing and being enlightened. While these are important concepts for us to latch onto, eventually we come to a place where we don't think about them anymore. We shouldn't have to; if the dynamics of our practice are in place, growth happens on its own. If you plant a seed in a place where there is enough moisture and nutrients and a little bit of sunlight, all those things come together and growth happens. You don't have to tell the seed to grow every day.

Surrendering is basically suspending everything—our thoughts, our emotions, our hopes,
our fears—suspending everything to create within ourselves a very big and simple environment
that allows us to be filled with something which
is very much higher and finer. We can think of it
as grace, we can think of it as love, we can think
of it as being filled with enlightenment.

If we continue to practice surrender, we find that
our lives are completely permeated by magic and
love, that every moment is a moment of joy and
every act is a manifestation of beauty. ∾

Liberation

∾ Liberation, enlightenment, freedom, perfection, salvation, whatever word we use, it is a state of being whose mere possibility has attracted and challenged people everywhere throughout recorded history. All spiritual and religious traditions have their own examples of people who have lived in this state. Such people come from all walks of life, all races and cultures, and all corners of the world.

∾ Liberation is always and only inside each person. It is really that dynamic stillness in which there is no external identification, but only all-pervasive pure awareness. There is no prerequisite for attaining perfection other than a total commitment and one-pointed devotion to attaining the highest state possible.

Being at rest even as we move and promoting the highest best interest of all people even as we live in stillness, this is the attainment of the recognition of our own total unity with God. This is also called liberation.

There is nothing we can acquire from outside which will make us beautiful and happy. Our own fulfillment comes only from within. Perfection is already inside us. What we have to do is get out of the way so it can happen.

Does enlightenment happen in a flash, or over a long period of time? The answer is yes. It happens in a flash, and it takes a lifetime for that flash to work its way through the entire field of our experience.

Liberation is being released from our mental entanglements, our desires, the whole complex of what we think we are and what we think we need and want. It is just to be quiet within ourselves and open. Liberation is not achieved after a long period of time. It is achieved instantaneously.

What takes a long period of time is for that state to become strong enough within us that we are stable in it, that we are not vacillating between states. We may become quiet and open a million times before we recognize that a very significant shift takes place within us every time we do that. Or we may recognize that it is a significant shift and not be able to sustain it for one reason or another. Still, it is a very simple thing. We continue to practice so that over time that state can gather more and more energy and become a self-reinforcing phenomenon. But liberation itself is not a long process; it's quick.

The essence of liberation is a real change of identity; we no longer think of ourselves as this individual person. Of course we operate through our bodies; this is the instrument that we have been given to play in articulating our piece of the symphony of life. But we no longer think that we are doing this thing and feeling that thing; we no longer think that there is something important about the doing and the feeling.

With the change of identity comes the recognition that the song we sing is really the song of God, not our song, and our actions are really the actions of the creative energy. This change of identity is a profound and sacred experience.

To achieve liberation we must have total commitment to leading a spiritual life. We work so deeply at it that we are put in direct and palpable contact with the essence of our own life which is the Essence of all life. We must practice deeply and long enough in contact with that Essence that we literally, totally merge into it; that's what we become. That is liberation.

Realization equals depth over time. Depth has everything to do with surrendering the struggle. It has to do with living first in contact with the flow and then in contact with the source of the flow which is vital force.

Perfection is not a state in which you arrive knowing all the answers to every question. Perfection is a state where upon arriving you experience complete happiness and complete peace just as you are.

Enlightenment isn't going to mysteriously dawn on us just because we do our spiritual practices every day. It only happens because we cause it to happen by the intentional one-pointedness of our energy. It happens through our devotion and commitment to leading a truly spiritual life.

To be in that state of liberation is to be in every way transcendent to suffering without in any sense being detached from our own humanness, or the needs of other human beings. We do not isolate ourselves or become insulated from the suffering that is around us. We live in a state which is intimately interconnected with the whole of life — interconnected, but in no way entangled in it.

Liberation is a state which is beyond transformation. It is not in any way separate or disconnected from other states of being. Rather, it is a transcendence and an encompassing of all other states. It exists in total contact.

Attaining perfect clarity and total peace within ourselves is not complicated or hard. The experience of freedom is a very pure, delicious, wonderful experience. It is very simple. We don't have to be rocket scientists or geniuses. The complexity is in our own minds. The hardness is in our own hearts.

We should think carefully about our spiritual work and to the best of our ability, with as much devotion and commitment as we can, authentically aspire to the state of total realization. This is an endeavor that is worth a lifetime.

The experience of God-realization is really communion with God. It is to be so completely one-pointed in our connection with the highest that we actually merge into That. Then we go beyond the perception of duality to experience all things as one thing; we go beyond coming and going, beyond being born and dying, beyond gain and loss. We see ourselves in everything and everything in ourselves. This awakening puts an end to fear, because if there is only one thing then what do we have to be afraid of? Thus we come to understand that the fundamental source of all energy in the world is also our own source. To understand this is to enter into a state of total well-being. ∾